THE UNOFFICIAL GUIDE TO
PROBLEM SOLVING IN MINECRAFT

JILL KEPPELER

Published in 2026 by The Rosen Publishing Group, Inc.
2544 Clinton Street, Buffalo, NY 14224

Copyright © 2026 by The Rosen Publishing Group, Inc.

All rights reserved. No part of this book may be reproduced in any form without permission in writing from the publisher, except by a reviewer.

First Edition

Editor: Greg Roza
Book Design: Rachel Rising
Illustrator: Matías Lapegüe

Photo Credits: Cover, pp. 1, 3–24 SkillUp/Shutterstock.com; Cover, p. 1 Soloma/Shutterstock.com; Cover, pp. 1, 3, 4, 6, 8, 10, 12, 15, 17, 18, 22, 23, 24 gersamina donnichi/Shutterstock.com; Cover, pp. 1, 3, 4, 6, 8, 10, 12, 15, 17, 18, 22, 23, 24 Oksana Kalashnykova/Shutterstock.com; p. 9 Prostock-studio/Shutterstock.com.

Library of Congress Cataloging-in-Publication Data

Names: Keppeler, Jill author
Title: The unofficial guide to problem solving in Minecraft / Jill
  Keppeler.
Description: [Buffalo] : PowerKids Press, [2026] | Series: Unofficial guide
  to Minecraft social skills | Includes index.
Identifiers: LCCN 2025015763 (print) | LCCN 2025015764 (ebook) | ISBN
  9781499452945 library binding | ISBN 9781499452938 paperback | ISBN
  9781499452952 ebook
Subjects: LCSH: Problem solving in children–Juvenile literature | Problem
  solving–Juvenile literature | Social skills in children–Juvenile
  literature | Minecraft (Game)–Juvenile literature
Classification: LCC BF723.P8 K47 2026 (print) | LCC BF723.P8 (ebook) |
  DDC 155.4/1343–dc23/eng/20250421
LC record available at https://lccn.loc.gov/2025015763
LC ebook record available at https://lccn.loc.gov/2025015764

Manufactured in the United States of America

Minecraft is a trademark of Mojang (a game development studio owned by Microsoft Technology Corporation), and its use in this book does not imply a recommendation or endorsement of this title by Mojang or Microsoft.

Some of the images in this book illustrate individuals who are models. The depictions do not imply actual situations or events.

CPSIA Compliance Information: Batch #CSPK26. For Further Information contact Rosen Publishing at 1-800-237-9932.

CONTENTS

JUST LIKE LIFE................	4
BIG AND SMALL	6
TAKING STEPS	8
BRAINSTORMING	10
CHECKING THE LIST	14
FAILURE IS ALWAYS AN OPTION ..	16
COMBINING IDEAS............	18
A PLAN COMES TOGETHER	20
GLOSSARY..................	22
FOR MORE INFORMATION	23
INDEX.....................	24

JUST LIKE LIFE

At times, life is smooth. There are no problems and no conflicts. You can do what you want, and nothing gets in your way. This can be great! But often, life isn't so smooth. You'll have to deal with trouble and solve, or fix, problems. It might not be as much fun, but it's part of life.

Gaming can be a lot like life! *Minecraft*, in which you can make a lot of your own decisions, is very much like this. You'll have to solve problems and figure things out. And if you're playing with friends, there are even more things to think about.

MINECRAFT MANIA

In a *Minecraft* world in creative **mode**, you can't get hurt, have unlimited **resources**, and can fly. In a survival world, though, you can get hurt and need to eat. More problems to solve!

Even in a *Minecraft* creative game, there will be problems to solve. If you're building a base, you'll need to find a good spot. You'll need to clear the land to have enough room.

BIG AND SMALL

Sometimes, your *Minecraft* problems (like real-world problems) will be big. How will you make it through the first night when all the monsters come out? What do you do if you get lost and can't find a way back to your base? What if the friends you're playing with can't get along?

These things are very important, but there are smaller problems too. What if you can't find the resources to upgrade your weapons? What if you can't find a good food source? What if a friend isn't working well with others? Sometimes, the small problems will be part of the bigger problems.

MINECRAFT MANIA

 The first sword you make in *Minecraft* will probably be a wooden sword. This will take two wooden planks and a stick. A stone sword is a little stronger. This takes two stone blocks and a stick.

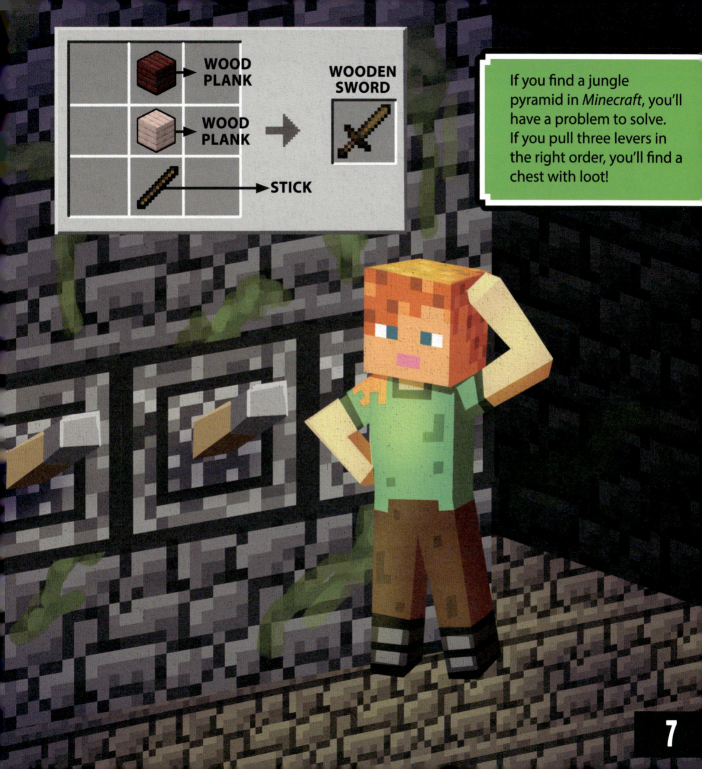

	WOOD PLANK			WOODEN SWORD
	WOOD PLANK	→		
	STICK			

If you find a jungle pyramid in *Minecraft*, you'll have a problem to solve. If you pull three levers in the right order, you'll find a chest with loot!

TAKING STEPS

With every problem, big or small, there will be steps toward solving it. It can be much easier if you break the problem down into these steps first. If not, really big problems could **overwhelm** you. Smaller problems, even if there are more of them, can be easier to manage.

First, clearly **identify** what the problem is. This might seem easy. Still, give it some thought. For example, you might think your problem is that one friend is using TNT to blow up others' bases. But what if you find out that they did this because the others took their supplies, and they want to get them back?

MINECRAFT MANIA

Minecraft TNT isn't just used in problems like this! You can also use it to clear land and flatten ground for building. You need five pieces of gunpowder and four blocks of sand to make one block of TNT.

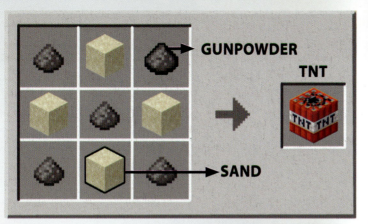

In another *Minecraft* example, maybe you keep getting lost. But is the problem really that you keep getting **distracted** while you explore?

BRAINSTORMING

Your first step is to brainstorm solutions, or fixes, for your problem. To brainstorm means to think about the problem and come up with ideas. At first, don't worry too much about how well those ideas will work! Write them all down. What may seem like a strange solution at first might wind up being the one that works best.

For example, if creepers keep blowing up part of your base, one thing you might write on a list of solutions could be: Get some pet cats. This might sound odd! But *Minecraft* creepers avoid cats. They'll run away if they see one.

MINECRAFT MANIA

You can find *Minecraft* cats in villages and swamp huts. You can tame them with some kinds of raw fish. Then they'll follow you and may bring you gifts like string, feathers, or raw chicken.

Try to be creative when you brainstorm. As in the example with the creepers and the cats, you never know what might work best. And don't just go with the first solution you think of. Keep brainstorming things and writing them down until you have at least a handful of ideas. This will help you think about the problem in different ways to come up with different solutions.

Other things you might write down about your creeper problem could include: Build a base that's all obsidian. Build another wall around your base. Light up the space between them really well. (Creepers only **spawn** when it's dark.)

MINECRAFT MANIA

 Obsidian is both a real-world material and a block in *Minecraft*. It has one of the highest blast resistances in the game. This is how much it can resist, or stand up to, explosions.

If a creeper gets within three blocks of a player, it will stop and start to hiss. After 1.5 seconds, it will blow up!

CHECKING THE LIST

Once you have your list of solutions, read through it again and think about every option, or choice. Think about things in favor of and against every item. A base made of obsidian would be nearly creeper-proof! It's very dark and shiny and looks cool too.

But it can be a challenge to find enough obsidian. Most of it will be deep underground. This can be dangerous, and you might have to do a lot of mining. Another way to find obsidian is to look for ruined **portals** on the surface. These structures look like portals to the Nether **dimension** but are missing some obsidian blocks.

MINECRAFT MANIA

You also can set up a way to make obsidian with water and lava. The lava must flow over a water **source**. This can be dangerous too, because lava will burn you.

A full Nether portal needs at least 10 blocks of obsidian. Light the middle with a flint and steel tool to create the portal.

FAILURE IS ALWAYS AN OPTION

So, let's say that you decide to build an obsidian base anyway. You set out to find enough of the stone. After a good bit of traveling, you find a ruined portal. But wait! You forgot that you need at least a diamond pickaxe to mine this stone. If you don't have one, you'll need to look for diamonds first. Diamonds are also found deep underground. You're back at square one.

An important part of problem solving is knowing that sometimes, the solution you pick first won't work. What's important is that you understand this and go back to your list to try something new.

MINECRAFT MANIA

 It will take 9.4 seconds to mine a block of obsidian with a diamond pickaxe. That's compared to 0.4 seconds to mine a block of cobblestone.

Ruined portals may also have stone, netherrack, lava, gold, and magma blocks around them.

COMBINING IDEAS

Look at your list again. Building another wall around your base can keep creepers away from your main base. If they blow up, you can just rebuild your wall! Look at your other options too. You don't have to use just one idea. You can light up the space between the wall and the main base as well. Otherwise, creepers could spawn in that space.

If you can, you could even add more ideas. If you know where there's a nearby village, you could go tame a few cats too. And when you're further in the game, you could still decide to go find some obsidian!

MINECRAFT MANIA

Creepers and many other **hostile** mobs spawn in the dark. This is why many of them appear at night. Creepers, however, don't die in the sunlight like some other monsters.

A PLAN COMES TOGETHER

After you've completed your problem solving, look back and think about it. What worked? What didn't? Keep this in mind the next time you need to solve a problem.

If you're playing with friends, of course, you'll probably need to have more people involved in problem solving at times. This can be great because it gives you more ideas, but it can be a problem if no one can agree on what solutions to try. Talk about what options seem best, then try them out. If they don't work, try other options. Be open to ideas from everyone!

GLOSSARY

dimension: A level of existence.

distract: To draw away attention.

hostile: Unfriendly or attacking. In Minecraft, it describes a mob that will always attack players.

identify: To figure out what something or someone is.

mode: A version, or form of something that is different from others.

overwhelm: To overpower with a great amount.

portal: A door or entrance.

resource: Something that can be used.

source: Where something comes from. In Minecraft, a water or lava source block is one that keeps producing more water or lava.

spawn: To first appear.

FOR MORE INFORMATION

BOOKS

Klimchuk, David. *You Can Fix It: Solving Problems*. PowerKids Press: Buffalo, NY, 2019.

Mojang AB. *Minecraft: Blockopedia*. Del Rey: New York, NY, 2021.

Mojang AB. *Minecraft: Mobspotter's Encyclopedia*. New York, NY: Random House Worlds, 2023.

WEBSITES

Brainstorming
www.niu.edu/citl/resources/guides/instructional-guide/brainstorming.shtml
Northern Illinois University Center for Innovative Teaching and Learning presents information about brainstorming to solve problems.

Creeper
minecraft.wiki/w/Creeper
Learn more about the classic mob on the Minecraft Wiki.

Publisher's note to educators and parents: Our editors have carefully reviewed these websites to ensure that they are suitable for students. Many websites change frequently, however, and we cannot guarantee that a site's future contents will continue to meet our high standards of quality and educational value. Be advised that students should be closely supervised whenever they access the internet.

INDEX

B

base, 4, 8, 10, 11, 12, 16, 18

brainstorm, 10, 12

C

cats, 10, 11, 12, 18

creeper, 10, 11, 12, 13, 14, 18, 19

conflict, 4

E

explosion, 12, 19

F

friends, 4, 6, 8, 20

L

leadership, 21

O

obsidian, 12, 14, 15, 16, 17, 18

options, 14, 16, 18, 20

P

portals, 14, 15, 16, 17

S

solution, 10, 12, 14, 16, 20

steps, 8

V

village, 10, 18